JESUS FEEDS THE 5,000

By Mark Ammerman
Illustrations by Ron Wheeler

One day Jesus and His best friends sailed in their boat to their favorite quiet place along the green grassy shore of the Sea of Galilee.

But when they got to their quiet place, it wasn't very quiet! A great big, loud crowd was already there. They wanted to meet Jesus.

When Jesus saw the crowd, He loved them very much. He talked to them all day long and healed everyone who was sick.

Finally, His best friends said to Him, "It's getting late and everyone is hungry. Send them to the nearest town to buy themselves some supper."

Jesus said, "They don't need to go away. You can give them supper."

But Jesus' friends didn't like that idea at all. "Do we have to spend all our own money to go buy them food?" they complained.

"How much bread did you bring with you?"
Jesus asked.

"All we have are five loaves of barley bread and two fish!" they said. "That's not enough for all these people!"

"Bring Me the food," said Jesus. Then He told the great big, loud, hungry crowd to sit down quietly on the grassy green shore.

Jesus took the five loaves and the two fish and looked up to heaven. He blessed the food and broke the loaves into pieces.

Jesus gave the pieces of bread to His best friends,
and they began to pass the bread out to all the
people who were sitting there.

Then Jesus broke the two fish into pieces and gave them to His friends.

This will never be enough for everyone, they thought.

"This is good bread," said some, "but there are too many people here!"

"This is good fish," said others, "but surely not enough to feed us all."

But as the bread and fish were passed around,
everyone broke off pieces large enough to eat.
And the food was passed from person to person.

Even though thousands of people were sitting on the hill, everyone got plenty of bread and fish! Everyone was fed! Everyone was full!

And when the meal was done, so much bread and fish were left over that the extra pieces filled up twelve big baskets!

Then Jesus told the great big, loud, stuffed crowd
that it was time for them to quietly go home.
And they all went home.

Then He sent His best friends back home, too.
They got in their boat and sailed out onto
the sea.

And when night came, Jesus went up into the mountain alone to pray.